EASY VAIL
35251002336434
12y
Vail, Grace
Dolphin doubbles

FEB - - 2014

Animal Math

Dolphin Doubles

By Grace Vail

Please visit our website, www.garethstevens.com. For a free color catalog of all our high-quality books, call toll free 1-800-542-2595 or fax 1-877-542-2596.

Library of Congress Cataloging-in-Publication Data

Vail, Grace.
Dolphin doubles / by Grace Vail.
   p. cm. — (Animal math)
Includes index.
ISBN 978-1-4339-9303-9 (pbk.)
ISBN 978-1-4339-9304-6 (6-pack)
ISBN 978-1-4339-9306-0 (library binding)
1. Arithmetic—Juvenile literature. 2. Addition—Juvenile literature. 3. Dolphins—Juvenile literature. I. Vail, Grace. II. Title.
QA115.V35 2013
513.211—dc23

First Edition

Published in 2014 by
Gareth Stevens Publishing
111 East 14th Street, Suite 349
New York, NY 10003

Copyright © 2014 Gareth Stevens Publishing

Designer: Katelyn E. Reynolds
Editor: Therese M. Shea

Photo credits: Cover, p. 1 Hemera/Thinkstock.com; pp. 3–24 (background texture) Natutik/Shutterstock.com; p. 5 Thomas Skjaeveland/Shutterstock.com; p. 6 iStockphoto/Thinkstock.com; pp. 7, 8, 13, 19 Mike Price/Shutterstock.com; p. 9 Xavier MARCHANT/Shutterstock.com; p. 11 Willyam Bradberry/Shutterstock.com; pp. 12, 14 Ramon grosso dolarea/Shutterstock.com; p. 15 Chris Curtis/Shutterstock.com; p. 16 BlueMoonStore/Shutterstock.com; p. 17 Alexander Chaikin/Shutterstock.com; p. 20 Kaththea/Shutterstock.com; p. 21 Tatyana Vychegzhanina/Shutterstock.com.

All rights reserved. No part of this book may be reproduced in any form without permission in writing from the publisher, except by a reviewer.

Printed in the United States of America

CPSIA compliance information: Batch #CD13GS: For further information contact Gareth Stevens, New York, New York at 1-800-542-2595.

Contents

Doubles Dolphin Fun 4

Blowholes. 6

Flippers, Flukes, Fins 8

Kinds of Dolphins. 10

Dolphin Talk. 16

Dolphin Pods 18

Playful and Smart 20

Glossary. 22

Answer Key 22

For More Information. 23

Index 24

Boldface words appear in the glossary.

Doubles Dolphin Fun

Dolphins aren't fish. They're **mammals**. They can help us with math. Dolphins make adding doubles fun!

2 dolphins + 2 dolphins = 4 dolphins

5

Blowholes

A dolphin has a **blowhole** on its head. The blowhole opens when a dolphin swims up to get air. It closes when a dolphin goes under the water.

```
  3 dolphins
+ 3 dolphins
-------------
  6 dolphins
```

7

Flippers, Flukes, Fins

A dolphin has two **flippers**. It has a tail fin called a fluke. Most dolphins have a fin on their back, too.

$$\begin{array}{r} 4 \text{ dolphins} \\ + \ 4 \text{ dolphins} \\ \hline 8 \text{ dolphins} \end{array}$$

9

Kinds of Dolphins

Marine dolphins live in oceans. There are river dolphins, too.

We can subtract doubles. Look at these 5 marine dolphins. How many are left if 5 swim away?

5 dolphins − 5 dolphins = 0 dolphins

11

Bottlenose dolphins are marine dolphins. They're gray. They have a short beak, or mouth. They swim in warm waters.

Which number sentence adds up to 10? (Check your answer on page 22.)

4 + 4   5 + 5

13

Killer whales aren't whales. They're the largest dolphins! Killer whales are also called orcas.

```
  3 killer whales
+ 3 killer whales
------------------
  6 killer whales
```

15

Dolphin Talk

Dolphins make noises like clicks and **whistles**. Some noises help them find food. Others are how they talk!

```
  6 dolphins
+ 6 dolphins
------------
 12 dolphins
```

17

Dolphin Pods

Some dolphins live in small groups called pods. Other dolphins live in larger groups called herds.

There are 6 dolphins. How many dolphins have to swim away so none are left?

19

Playful and Smart

Dolphins are smart. They learn to do tricks. Some even help people. Dolphins love to play—just like you!

Use the pictures to write a doubles number sentence. How many dolphins are there in all?

21

Glossary

blowhole: a body part on the top of the head of a dolphin or other sea animal that allows it to breathe

flipper: an animal's wide, flat body part that is used for swimming

mammal: an animal that has a backbone and hair, breathes air, and feeds milk to its young

whistle: to make a sound by blowing breath through lips or teeth

Answer Key

page 12:
5 + 5

page 18:
6 dolphins

page 20:
4 + 4 = 8
8 dolphins

For More Information

Books

Freese, Joan. *Doubles Fun on the Farm.* Pleasantville, NY: Weekly Reader Publishing, 2008.

Riggs, Kate. *Dolphins.* Mankato, MN: Creative Education, 2012.

Simon, Seymour. *Dolphins.* New York, NY: HarperCollins, 2009.

Websites

Basic Facts About Dolphins
www.defenders.org/dolphin/basic-facts
Read how dolphins use sounds to find their way.

Killer Whale (Orca)
animals.nationalgeographic.com/animals/mammals/killer-whale/
Learn more about these large dolphins and their underwater lives.

Ladybird Doubles
www.maths-games.org/ladybird-doubles.html
Play a memory game while adding doubles.

Publisher's note to educators and parents: Our editors have carefully reviewed these websites to ensure that they are suitable for students. Many websites change frequently, however, and we cannot guarantee that a site's future contents will continue to meet our high standards of quality and educational value. Be advised that students should be closely supervised whenever they access the Internet.

Index

beak 12
blowhole 6
bottlenose dolphins 12
clicks 16
fin 8
flippers 8
fluke 8
herds 18
killer whales 14
mammals 4
marine dolphins 10, 12
oceans 10
orcas 14
play 20
pods 18
river dolphins 10
tail fin 8
tricks 20
whistles 16